Jack Russell Terrier

Bundle of Energy

by Natalie Lunis

Consultant: Michael Bilbo
Member of the Jack Russell Terrier Club
of America Board of Directors
and a JRTCA Sanctioned Working Judge

BEARPORT
PUBLISHING

New York, New York

Credits

Cover and Title Page, © Mike Bilbo; TOC, © Eric Isselée/Shutterstock; 4, © Mike Bilbo; 5, © Mike Bilbo; 6, © Mike Bilbo; 7, © Mike Bilbo; 8, © Mary Evans Picture Library; 9L, © Juniors Bildarchiv; 9R, © Coughlin Studio; 10, Permission courtesy of Mrs. C. Poortvliet-Bouman, from the book *Dogs* by Rien Poortvliet; 11T, © Juniors Bildarchiv/ Alamy; 11BL, © Mark Raycroft; 11BR, © Dusan Smetana; 12, © The Hunt, 1920s (oil on canvas), Wright, Gilbert Scott (1880-1958)/Private Collection/The Bridgeman Art Library; 13, © Klein J.-L. & Hubert M.-L./Biosphoto/Peter Arnold Inc.; 14, © E.A. Janes/age fotostock/SuperStock; 15L, © Michael Boys/Corbis; 15R, © Les Wilson/Rex Features; 16L, © Frank Lukasseck/age fotostock/SuperStock; 16R, © Mark Raycroft; 17, © Juniors Bildarchiv/Alamy; 18, © Plush Studios/Getty Images/Punchstock; 19T, © Aaron M. Sprecher/epa/Corbis; 19BL, © Chris Butler/age fotostock/SuperStock; 19BR, © David Hartley/Rex Features; 20, © Kaisa Siren/Rex Features; 21, © Dusan Smetana; 22, © Ariel Skelley/Corbis; 23T, © Juniors Bildarchiv/Alamy; 23B, © John Stillwell/PA Archive/PA Photos; 24, © NBCU Photo Bank; 25T, Courtesy of Big Feats Entertainment; 25B, © The Granger Collection, New York; 26, © Mike Blake/Reuters/ Landov; 27, © Barry Batchelor/PA Archive/PA Photos; 28, © Dusan Smetana; 29, © Mike Bilbo; 31, © Mike Bilbo; 32, © Eric Isselée/Shutterstock.

Publisher: Kenn Goin
Editorial Director: Adam Siegel
Creative Director: Spencer Brinker
Photo Researcher: Daniella Nilva
Design: Dawn Beard Creative

Library of Congress Cataloging-in-Publication Data

Lunis, Natalie.
  Jack Russell terrier : bundle of energy / by Natalie Lunis.
    p. cm. — (Little dogs rock!)
  Includes bibliographical references and index.
  ISBN-13: 978-1-59716-747-5 (library binding)
  ISBN-10: 1-59716-747-9 (library binding)
  1. Jack Russell terrier—Juvenile literature. I. Title.
  SF429.J27L86 2009
  636.755—dc22
                              2008040487

For more information, write to Bearport Publishing Company, Inc., 101 Fifth Avenue, Suite 6R, New York, New York 10003. Printed in the United States of America.

10 9 8 7 6 5 4 3 2 1

Contents

Into the Tunnel

"Find the rat! Find the rat!"

Darlene McInnes was speaking to her Jack Russell Terrier, Bisley, in an excited voice. Both of them were in a field near the entrance to a small tunnel. It was just big enough for Bisley to squeeze inside.

▲ **Bisley**

Bisley was excited, too. She could smell a rat that was nearby. Bisley quickly disappeared into the tunnel. Once inside, she managed to follow the rat's **scent** through the pitch-black darkness. In less than five seconds, she had found the caged animal at the end of the tunnel. Now she needed to do only one more thing at this Jack Russell Terrier **trial** in order to win the title of Go-to-Ground Champion.

▲ A Jack Russell Terrier entering a tunnel to find a rat

Jack Russell Terriers are called Jack Russells, Jacks, or JRTs for short.

Passing the Test

Bisley needed to "work" the rat for 60 seconds. That meant barking and **whining** to let people know where it was, as well as digging near the rat's cage. As soon as she passed the test, a judge would remove Bisley from the tunnel and record her score. If Bisley's time was better than all the other dogs' times, then the judge would award Bisley her title.

▲ **Bisley working the rat**

Jack Russell Terrier trials are fun and exciting for JRTs like Bisley. However, they are more than just a way of getting outdoors for lots of exercise. The trials are also a way for Jack Russell Terriers to show that they still have the skills to do the job they were first raised for—hunting **pests** that hide in **dens** or tunnels dug into the earth.

▲ **A rat at a Jack Russell Terrier trial**

The pet rats that are used during Jack Russell Terrier trials are not harmed. Most get used to being "worked" by the barking dogs. In fact, many of the rats even take a nap during the whole event.

The Sporting Parson

Jack Russell Terriers got their start in England during the early 1800s. The person who developed the **breed** was John Russell, also known as Jack. Russell served as the **parson** of a country church. Whenever he wasn't working, he loved being out in the countryside enjoying his favorite hobby—fox hunting.

Parson Jack Russell

Jack Russell loved fox hunting and other outdoor activities so much that people called him the "sporting parson."

Russell loved dogs, too—especially hunting dogs. One day he saw a little white dog named Trump. He thought that she would be the perfect dog for following foxes into their **burrows** during a hunt, and he bought her right away. Soon he started raising dogs that had her best **traits**. Over time, the dogs came to be known as Jack Russell Terriers.

Trump

A Jack Russell Terrier today

The first Jack Russell Terriers were raised about 200 years ago in England.

The Right Size and Color

Jack Russell was right. Trump turned out to be the perfect dog to hunt foxes. She was the same size as a fox, so she could fit herself into a burrow. She had a strong chest and strong front legs, so she could dig her way through any tight spots she found underground.

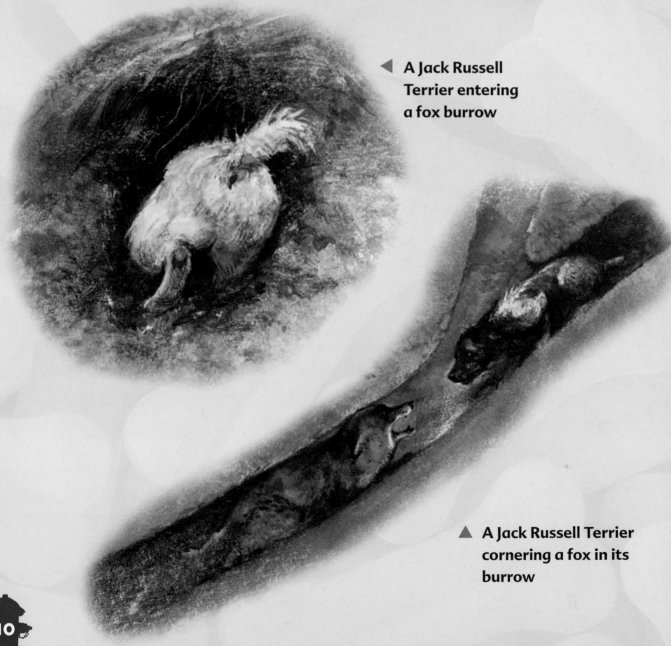

◄ **A Jack Russell Terrier entering a fox burrow**

▲ **A Jack Russell Terrier cornering a fox in its burrow**

Trump's **coat** also helped her in her job as a hunting dog. Since the coat was mainly white, hunters and other dogs would not mistake her for a fox. It was also rough and wiry, which helped protect her from rain and from rough branches and sharp **thorns**.

Today, Jack Russell Terriers come in three different kinds of coats. Some have rough, wiry coats like Trump's. Others have smooth ones. The most common coat, however, is one that is between rough and smooth, called broken.

rough coat

smooth coat

broken coat

A Tough Dog for a Tough Job

The Jack Russell Terrier wasn't just the right size and color for hunting foxes. It had the right personality, too.

To face a fox in its underground hiding place, the little dog needed to be tough, smart, and brave. It also needed to be lively and full of energy to keep up with the hunters, who rode on horseback alongside fast-running, long-legged **foxhounds**.

During a hunt, foxhounds followed the trail of a fox by sensing its smell.

Jack Russells also had to be loyal to their human owners. At the same time, they had to have an **independent** streak. Otherwise, they would not be able to think and act on their own when they went underground after foxes.

Jack Russell Terriers were expected to be **bold** and daring but not **vicious**. Their job was to scare the fox out of a tunnel without hurting it. That way, hunters could continue to chase it.

More Jobs for Jacks

During Jack Russell's lifetime, JRTs became famous throughout England as hunting dogs. It didn't take long, however, for people to see that these little dogs were good at doing other kinds of jobs as well.

Over a period of time that stretched from the 1800s to the 1900s, Jack Russell Terriers became popular in the United States and Canada as farm dogs and as pets.

The Jack Russell's hunting ability made it an excellent "ratter"—that is, a dog that catches and kills rats. Farmers and owners of horse **stables** often had trouble with the big **rodents**. So they depended on Jack Russell Terriers to keep the problem under control.

Other people simply enjoyed the little white dog's adventurous, playful, and fun-loving spirit. They saw that it would make a great pet—for the right kind of owner.

▲ Rats find plenty of food and places to nest in barns. That's why farmers need Jack Russells and other pets to keep them away.

Some dogs are afraid of horses— but not Jack Russell Terriers. They get along well with the huge animals.

On the Move

Even the biggest Jack Russell fans will admit that their favorite dog is not for everyone. The little white terrier is no couch potato. It needs an owner who can keep up with its active lifestyle and make sure it has lots of places to play.

Jack Russells are among the most intelligent and curious of all dog breeds. They need games and activities that exercise their minds as well as their bodies.

▲ **Jack Russell Terriers are full of energy. They can crawl deep into the ground, and they can jump high into the air.**

Jack Russells need at least two hours of walking, running, and jumping every day. That's more workout time than most people are able to fit into their busy lives. The active little dogs also need a large yard as well as opportunities to explore new places, like a park, a lakeshore, or the woods. Otherwise, they will get bored and restless and start looking for ways to get into trouble.

Some small dogs can get all the exercise they need by moving around in an apartment or small yard. The Jack Russell isn't one of them.

Staying Out of Trouble

How much trouble can a cute little white dog get into? It can get into plenty—especially when it has strong **instincts** for hunting.

For example, as hunting dogs, Jack Russells were supposed to bark. Their barking scared foxes out of their burrows and let hunters know where the action was. As pets, Jacks often bark nonstop when they are bored. After all, it's something to do.

Some dogs, including Jack Russells, bark just for fun. They seem to like the sounds they make. This activity is called recreational barking.

Jacks also dug into tunnels and leaped over logs during hunts. Now they often dig under or jump over fences to escape from backyards. No wonder Jack Russell owners say that this is not a dog that should be left home alone all day—or even for just a few hours!

◄ In most places, Jack Russells need to walk on leashes. Otherwise, they might take off after a squirrel, chipmunk, or other small animal.

▼ Jack Russells like to explore and investigate while they are indoors, too.

◄ Always curious, Jack Russells can be eager to escape from yards in order to explore the outside world.

Junior Jacks

Like young children, puppies are playful, curious, and sometimes **mischievous**. People who bring puppies into their homes have to take steps to make sure their little pets don't wreck the house or hurt themselves. For example, they need to hide items that a puppy might mistake for food, like medicines and soaps. They also need to keep electric cords out of the way, so the puppies don't chew them and get a bad shock.

Puppies will play with and chew on just about anything, so their owners need to keep an eye on them.

Jack Russell puppies are even more mischievous than many other kinds of young dogs. So their owners have to be even more careful when they **puppy-proof** their homes. Little Jacks love to dig, so their owners need to keep indoor plants out of the way. Outdoors, they need good fences to make sure the yards are escape-proof.

Eight-week-old Jack Russell Terrier puppies

Most kinds of puppies, including Jack Russells, are ready to be **adopted** as pets when they are about eight weeks old.

Friends and Enemies

Jack Russells are loyal and loving toward their human families. They get along well with children, as long as the children show them kindness and respect. That means not squeezing them, dropping them, or suddenly grabbing toys away from them.

▲ **These young Jack Russell Terrier owners know how to keep their dog clean.**

How do Jacks get along with other pets? It depends on the kind of animal. At the top of the list are other Jacks. The best combination is one male and one female per home. At the bottom of the list are small animals like hamsters and guinea pigs. The dogs will probably think of them as **prey** and try to hunt them. Somewhere in the middle are cats. Some Jacks think of them as friends. Others think they look like foxes and treat them as animals to be hunted.

Jack Russells are more likely to get along with cats if they get used to being around them as puppies. When a puppy gets older, however, it may decide that the cat is fun to hunt.

▲ **Sometimes Jack Russells make friends with dogs of other breeds, such as this French mastiff.**

Star Power

Some Jack Russells have found success in show business—especially as TV stars. One of the best known is Moose, the real dog behind the TV character Eddie on *Frasier*. Another is Soccer, who from 1995 to 1998 played Wishbone in the children's television series of the same name.

▲ *Frasier* was a popular TV comedy that ran from 1993 to 2004. In this picture, the cast poses with Moose (Eddie).

Seeing these cute, funny, and smart **canine** stars made lots of fans want to have their own JRTs. However, the dogs' trainers often remind people that it takes many, many hours of practice to get them to behave like hard-working actors. Behind the scenes, they act like real Jack Russells—always full of energy, and often full of mischief, too.

In every episode, TV's Wishbone ▶ imagined he was taking part in an adventure from a classic book, such as *The Adventures of Robin Hood*.

A Jack Russell Terrier is featured in one of the most famous magazine ads of all time. The ad, for the entertainment company RCA, was created more than 100 years ago.

In the RCA ad, a Jack Russell Terrier listens to a recording of his owner's voice.

VICTOR

Real-Life Adventures

Buddy and Freddie are two more Jack Russell Terriers that have appeared on TV and in magazines. They are not famous for playing make-believe parts, however. Instead, they are known for their real-life adventures.

Buddy is a canine surfer from California. He rides the waves twice a week with his owner and has even entered "surf dog" competitions.

Buddy often barks as he rides the waves.

Like all "surf dog" competitors, Buddy wears a life jacket for safety.

Freddie, a JRT from England, rides a pony. He first hopped on his friend Daisy when he saw a child getting ready to ride. After that, he started trotting around with Daisy two or three times a day.

These four-legged **daredevils** might surprise many people—but not Jack Russell owners. People who get to know these dogs know that they only look small. In their own minds, they're large and in charge!

Freddie and Daisy

Jack Russell Terriers at a Glance

Weight:	10–18 pounds (4.5–8 kg)
Height at Shoulder:	10–15 inches (25–38 cm)
Coat:	Smooth, rough, or broken
Colors:	White with black, tan, or brown markings, mainly on the head and near the tail
Country of Origin:	England
Life Span:	12–15 years
Personality:	Bold, friendly, active, and clever; likes to hunt, chase small animals, and explore outdoor places; digs a lot

Best in Show

What makes a great Jack Russell Terrier? Every owner knows that his or her dog is special. Judges in dog shows, however, look very carefully at a Jack Russell Terrier's appearance and behavior. Here are some of the things they look for:

ears are small and V-shaped and fall forward on the head

head is flat on top and fairly wide between the ears, narrowing to the eyes

neck is muscular and fairly long, becoming wider at the shoulders

eyes are dark and almond-shaped

chest should be fairly small and narrow

coat should be more than 51 percent white, with tan, black, or brown markings

front legs should be strong and straight-boned

back legs should be strong and muscular

Behavior:
lively, active, bold, and alert; should not be shy

29

Glossary

adopted (uh-DOPT-id) taken into a family

bold (BOHLD) daring

breed (BREED) a kind of dog

burrows (BUR-ohz) holes or tunnels in the ground made by an animal to live in

canine (KAY-nine) having to do with dogs

coat (KOHT) the fur on a dog or other animal

daredevils (DAIR-*dev*-ilz) people or animals that do dangerous or risky things

dens (DENZ) homes where wild animals can rest, hide from enemies, and have babies

foxhounds (FOKS-houndz) a kind of dog that is trained to use its sense of sight and smell to hunt foxes

independent (*in*-di-PEN-duhnt) able to do things without needing help from others

instincts (IN-stingkts) knowledge and ways of acting that an animal is born with

mischievous (MISS-chuh-vuhss) able to cause trouble, often through playful behavior

parson (PAR-suhn) minister of a church

pests (PESTS) animals that bother or annoy people

prey (PRAY) animals that are hunted for food

puppy-proof (PUP-ee-*proof*) to make safe for a puppy

rodents (ROH-duhnts) a group of animals with large front teeth that includes rats, mice, squirrels, and chipmunks

scent (SENT) a smell

stables (STAY-buhlz) the part of a building where horses or cows are kept

thorns (THORNZ) sharp points on the stems or branches of plants

traits (TRAYTS) ways of looking and acting

trial (TRYE-uhl) competition

vicious (VISH-uhss) violent and dangerous

whining (WINE-ing) making a high-pitched, crying-like sound

Bibliography

Brown, Catherine Romaine. *Jack Russell Terrier.* Hoboken, NJ: Wiley (2006).

Coile, D. Caroline. *The Jack Russell Terrier Handbook.* Hauppauge, NY: Barron's (2000).

Dunbar, Ian. *The Essential Jack Russell Terrier.* New York: Howell Book House (1998).

Read More

Green-Armytage, Stephen. *Dudley: The Little Terrier That Could.* New York: Scholastic (2000).

Murray, Julie. *Jack Russell Terriers.* Edina, MN: ABDO (2005).

Temple, Bob. *Jack Russell Terriers.* Edina, MN: ABDO (2000).

Learn More Online

To learn more about Jack Russell Terriers, visit
www.bearportpublishing.com/LittleDogsRock

Index

About the Author

Natalie Lunis has written many science and nature books for children. She lives in the Hudson River Valley, just north of New York City.